Trappers & Mountain Men

By Anastasia Suen

Content Advisor:
Jerome O. Steffen, Ph.D.
History Department
Georgia Southern University

Rourke

Publishing LLC
Vero Beach, Florida 32964

www.rourkepublishing.com

Image Credits:
Library of Congress, cover (top left, bottom right), 4, 6, 7,8 (right), 11, 13, 15 (top left and right), 16-17, 19, 20, 21, 22-23, 25 (bottom), 26, 27, 29, 32-33, 37, 38-39, 40, 43, 44 (third and fourth from top. 45 top), 46 (first column—first and third from top, second column—second, third, fourth, and fifth from top); iStockphoto, cover (bottom left), 5 (bottom), 8 (bottom left), 12, 42; Stock Montage, cover (top right), 10, 14-15, 25 (top right), 44 (top), 46 (first column—second from top, second column—first from top); North Wind Picture Archives, 9, 18, 34; Holt-Atherton Special Collections, University of the Pacific Library, 5, 45 (second from top)

Editorial Direction: Red Line Editorial, Inc.; Bob Temple

Editor: Nadia Higgins

Designer: Lindaanne Donohoe

Fact Research: Laurie Kahn

Library of Congress Cataloging-in-Publication Data

Suen, Anastasia.
  Trappers and mountain men / by Anastasia Suen
      p. cm.— (Events in American history)
  Audience: Grade 4–6.
  ISBN 1–60044–134–3 (hardcover)
  ISBN 978-1-60044-358-9 (paperback)
 1. Pioneers—West (U.S.)—History—19th century—Juvenile literature.
2. Trappers—West (U.S.)—History—19th century—Juvenile literature.
3. Explorers—West (U.S.)—History—19th century—Juvenile literature.
4. Frontier and pioneer life—West (U.S.)—Juvenile literature. 5. Fur trade—West (U.S.)—History—19th century—Juvenile literature. 6. West (U.S.)—History—To 1848—Juvenile literature. 7. West (U.S.)—Discovery and exploration—Juvenile literature. 8. West (U.S.)—Biography—Juvenile literature. I. Title.
  F592.S864 2007
  978'.02—dc22
                                    2006018730

Printed in the USA

Rourke
Publishing LLC
Vero Beach, Florida 32964

Table of Contents

Chapter One

Trappers and Mountain Men

It was the winter of 1824 and the snow just wouldn't let up. Neither would the wind. But a blizzard in the Rocky Mountains didn't stop Jedediah Smith's expedition. Smith and his men wanted to be trapping beavers in the mountains before the weather got too warm. A beaver's fur is thickest when the weather is cold.

Night after night, the wind blew out the men's fires. Some days, it was so cold, their hands went numb. When it was too cold to hold a flint and steel, they couldn't even start a fire.

"Although the wind blew and the fine frosty snow crept in and around us, this was not the worst, for the cold hard frozen earth on which we lay was still more disagreeable so that sleep was out of the Question."

James Clyman

Above: Jedediah Smith
Left: A beaver gnaws on a tree stump.

A mountain man looks out for danger.

The blizzard kept the wild animals away, but that meant there was no game to hunt. The men had nothing to eat. Smith and his men traveled through the blizzard for six days. Then James Clyman saw tracks. Would they eat at last?

Clyman and William Sublette started running. They followed the tracks in the snow until they saw a buffalo. Sublette counted to three, and both men fired. Then they reloaded and shot again.

Rocky Mountains in the winter

As the last shots rang out, the other men in their company arrived on the scene. Food at last! The mountain men were so hungry they cut up the dead buffalo then and there. It was too windy to make a fire, so they ate the meat raw.

After packing the rest of the meat, the men continued their journey. They didn't know it at the time, but they were crossing the South Pass. This route through the Rockies would change U.S. history.

Several days later, the mountain men reached their destination. They arrived at Green River. Here they would be able to trap beaver when the river thawed in the spring.

Beaver Hats

For 200 years, Europeans prized hats made from beaver fur. To make a beaver hat, the hatter, or hatmaker, plucked out the stiffer "guard" hairs. The hatter wanted only the soft fur underneath. Then the hatter brushed the fur with mercury. This made the fur stand up so the hatter could shave it. Once shaved, the beaver fur was called fluff.

The hatter would boil, roll, and stretch the fluff. Now the soft, smooth fur was called felt. The felt was then shaped into a hat.

Unfortunately, each time the felt was heated or moistened, it released mercury fumes. The hatter breathed in the fumes, and the mercury attacked his nervous system. Soon the hatter couldn't control his muscles or think and speak clearly. People didn't understand what caused the hatter's unusual behavior. Hatters seemed "mad," or insane. That's where the expression "mad as a hatter" comes from.

Left: Most often, beaver hats were not furry. The fur was pressed together into felt, as shown in this example. Above: An illustration from 1898 shows a girl wearing a hat and coat trimmed with beaver fur.

Mountain men were trappers who lived off wild land deep in the Rocky Mountains during the first half of the nineteenth century. They trapped beaver so that people in cities far away could wear hats made from the animal's fur. The trappers endured great hardships in pursuit of the prized beaver.

Even though mountain men seldom saw other people, they changed the lives of many. As they searched for beaver, the men traveled across regions that were unknown to most Americans. The maps they made of the lands they explored helped the United States grow. Settlers later used these maps to start new lives out West.

A beaver pelt

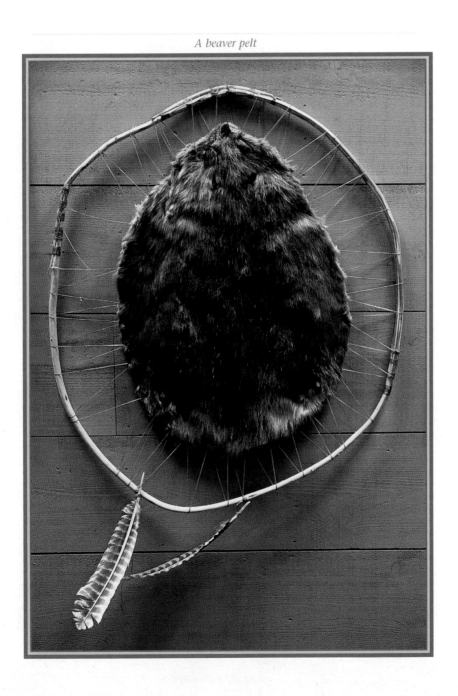

Chapter Two

Lewis and Clark's Journey

The story of the mountain men begins with the Louisiana Purchase, in 1803. The territory between the Mississippi River and the Rocky Mountains was made part of the United States, more than doubling the country's size. These lands held great promise for fur traders and trappers.

A portrait of Thomas Jefferson from 1800 shows him wearing a crown of leaves as a symbol of his greatness.

President Thomas Jefferson wanted to find out what was on the land he had bought, so he assembled a Corps of Discovery to explore the western territory. Meriwether Lewis led the expedition, with William Clark as second in command. Lewis and Clark put together a group of about 40 men who would travel with them from St. Louis to the Pacific Ocean and back.

As they traveled, the Corps would make maps and take notes about the people, animals, and plants they observed. They would return with a wealth of information, including the news that plenty of beavers were to be found deep in the wilderness of the Rocky Mountains.

The famous journey began in May 1804. The Corps of Discovery left from a town near St. Louis and went up the Missouri River. They were going against the flow of the river, so paddling their boats took extra effort. The journey took all spring, summer, and fall. Both Lewis and Clark kept journals of their discoveries. So did other members of their company. By winter, the Corps had reached North Dakota. They traded with the Mandan Indians, who allowed them to stay and build huts for the winter. Here they met Sacagawea, an Indian woman who would later help them.

"Should you reach the Pacific ocean inform yourself of the circumstances which may decide whether the furs of those parts may not be collected as advantageously at the head of the Missouri."

Thomas Jefferson, letter to Meriwether Lewis, June 20, 1803

Mandan Indians of North Dakota assisted the
Lewis and Clark expedition.

"Captain Lewis, through an interpreter,
delivered a speech; gave a suit
of clothes to each of the chiefs
and some articles for their villages. . . .
At three o'clock another gun was
fired at the breaking up of the council,
and they all appeared satisfied.
Captain Lewis gave an iron mill to
the Mandan nation to grind their corn,
with which they were highly pleased."

Sergeant Patrick Gass

When the weather warmed up, the Corps continued up the Missouri River until they reached its source in western Montana. It was in Montana that plans fell apart. For hundreds of years, explorers had been searching for what was called the Northwest Passage—a waterway that cut across North America to the Pacific Ocean. The Corps had high hopes of discovering the famous river. But all they found were miles and miles of mountains. Soon, the men would learn that these Rocky Mountains held other valuable resources—including plenty of beaver fur.

A map showing the route of the Louis and Clark expedition, from St. Louis to the Pacific Ocean (in present-day Oregon)

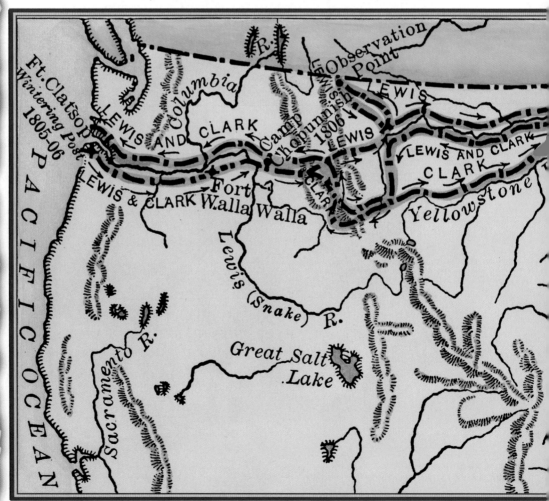

The Corps had to leave their boats behind. The only way they could travel across the mountains was to walk. But how could they carry all of their supplies? Sacagawea remembered that the Shoshone were nearby—and they had horses.

Left: Meriwether Lewis
Below: William Clark

"I soon obtained three very good horses, for which I gave a uniform coat, a pair of leggings, a few handkerchiefs, three knives and some other small articles the whole of which did not cost more than about 20$ in the U' States. The Indians seemed quite as well pleased with their bargain as I was."

Meriwether Lewis

With horses to carry the supplies, the Corps walked across the Rocky Mountains. They traveled about 150 miles (241 kilometers) before reaching the Clearwater River in Idaho. They had left their boats far behind, so the Corps cut down trees and built new ones. The Corps then sailed down the Clearwater to the Snake River. The Snake flowed into the Columbia River, which flowed into the Pacific Ocean. At last they had reached their destination!

The Corps of Discovery remained on the Pacific Coast that winter and began their return journey the following spring. They arrived back in St. Louis on September 23, 1806. They were hailed as heroes as they made their way to Washington, D.C. Soon everyone in St. Louis would know that beaver could be found in the Louisiana Territory.

The Snake River runs through present-day Wyoming and Idaho. Lewis and Clark explored the river during their famous expedition.

Chapter Three

Trapping Expeditions

Thomas Jefferson wasn't the only one interested in his country's new lands.

As the Corps was traveling back down the Missouri River to St. Louis, they encountered two men. It was very unusual to see white men so far upriver, so the Corps stopped to talk with them.

Joseph Dickson and Forest Hancock were in search of beaver. They swapped stories with the Corps and were quite happy to learn that beaver was plentiful where they were going.

"[T]he bowsman informed me that there was a canoe and a camp he believed of white men on the N.E. shore ... found it to be the camp of two hunters from the Illinois by name Joseph Dickson and Forest Hancock."

Meriwether Lewis

A drawing of a beaver from the 1840s

Friend or Foe?

When Lewis and Clark traveled with Sacagawea, it was easy to see that they were not a war party. War parties never traveled with a woman and her baby. Lewis and Clark's party was seen as a peaceful one.

The same cannot be said for the parties of trappers and traders that followed. These groups were all male. Some tribes were friendly to strangers and some were hostile. They didn't want strangers trapping in their area.

In 1809, John Colter was checking traps with his friend John Potts. Suddenly they were surrounded by hundreds of Blackfeet. Potts shot at the Indians, so they shot back. Potts died, and the Blackfeet seized Colter. Colter escaped into the wilderness. Seven days later, he arrived back at the fort, sunburned, bloody, and half-dead.

One member of the Corps, John Colter, decided to join them. He turned around and headed back into the wilderness with the trappers.

When Lewis and Clark arrived back in St. Louis, word of their travels spread. News about the abundance of beaver up the Missouri River was of particular interest to trappers and traders. In the spring of 1807, several parties set out from St. Louis to find beaver for themselves.

A 1912 statue of Sacagawea with her baby pays tribute to the explorer in City Park, Portland, Oregon.

"Colter, one of our men, expressed a desire to join some trappers. . . . We gave [John] Colter some small articles which we did not want and some powder and lead. The party also gave him several articles which will be useful to him on his expedition."

William Clark

Manuel Lisa, a fur trader from New Orleans, led the first such party up the Missouri. Several of the men in his company, including George Drouillard, had been members of the Corps of Discovery. When Lisa's group reached the Platte River, they recognized a man canoeing downstream. It was John Colter! Colter's knowledge of the territory would be very helpful to the expedition, so, once again, he returned to the wilderness.

In this 1866 painting, trappers rest around a campfire in the wilderness.

The men retraced Colter's route up the Platte River. When winter came the trappers and traders built a fort, which Lisa named after his son, Raymond. Fort Raymond also served as a trading post. Lisa sent Colter out to tell the nearby Indians that he would trade for beaver pelts. But Lisa also wanted his men to find beaver furs themselves.

"At the head of this river the natives give an account that there is frequently heard a loud noise, like Thunder, which makes the earth Tremble. They State that they seldom go there because their children Cannot sleep— and Conceive it possessed of spirits, who were averse that men Should be near them."

William Clark, describing the reaction of American Indians to the geysers at what is now Yellowstone National Park

An 1814 map shows the route of Lewis and Clark's journey. The map is a copy of one drawn by Clark himself.

A Map of LEWIS AND CLARK'S TRACK, Across the Western Portion of North America From the MISSISSIPPI to the PACIFIC OCEAN; By Order of the Executive of the UNITED STATES, in 1804.5.&6. Copied by Samuel Lewis from the Original Drawing of W. Clark.

Colter went on to discover the wonders of what is now Yellowstone National Park. His descriptions of boiling hot springs and geysers that came up out of the ground were so amazing that many people thought he had made them up.

John Colter and George Drouillard traversed the Rocky Mountains trapping beavers. In 1808, Drouillard made a map of the places he and Colter had traveled. After he returned to St. Louis, Drouillard showed his map to Clark, who was making a map based on his own travels. Clark added details from Drouillard's map to his own. Slowly, the mysteries of the West were being revealed.

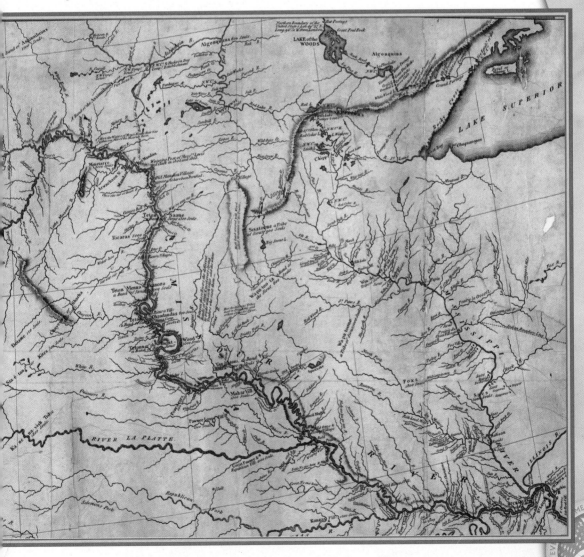

Chapter Four

John Jacob Astor's Fur-Trading Empire

John Jacob Astor was a businessman who had made a lot of money from the fur trade in northern New York and Canada. After Lewis and Clark's expedition, Astor saw a chance to make even more money trapping beaver in Oregon. So he started the Pacific Fur Company. In time, Astor would build a fur-trading empire that dominated the industry in the United States.

Opposite page: A fur-trading center set up by John Jacob Astor looks like a small village in the distance. Right: John Jacob Astor. Bottom: Astor's interest in the Oregon region was in making money. Later, as settlers began moving there, maps of the area, such as this one from 1841, were created.

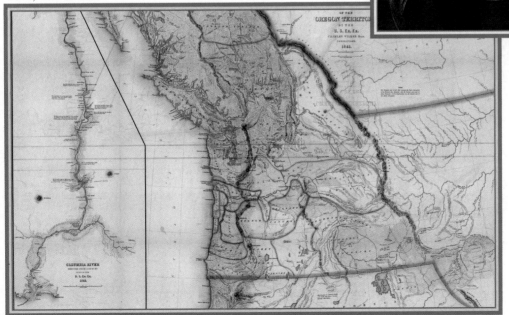

In 1810, Astor sent two crews out west. His men would meet a great deal of hardship—even tragedy—getting to Oregon. One crew went by sea, the other went by land. The ship *Tonquin* left New York City in September. It sailed around South America and picked up workers in Hawaii. The *Tonquin* reached the Columbia River in Oregon the following April, but the waters were so rough that eight crewmen drowned when they tried to land.

A photo of the Columbia River

Eventually some of the men went ashore to build a fort while the others remained on the ship. But their captain, Jonathan Thorn, was impatient to trade with the Indians, so the rest of crew sailed north. They invited a local tribe, the Salish, on board. Thorn's treatment of the Salish was so disrespectful that they retaliated by attacking their hosts. The entire crew was killed.

The workers building the outpost, which they called Fort Astoria, were having problems of their own. Catching beavers and selling their furs was not the same as building a fort in the wilderness. They didn't know how to do the work, and it showed.

"It would have made a cynic smile to see this pioneer corps, composed of traders, shopkeepers, voyageurs, and Owyhees (Hawaiians), all ignorant alike in this new walk of life, and the most ignorant of all, the leader. Many of the party had never handled an axe before, and but few of them knew how to use a gun, but necessity, the mother of invention, soon taught us both."

Alexander Ross,
a member of Astor's crew

A 1910 illustration shows Salish Indians in Montana. The Salish clashed with Astor's men in the eary 1800s.

Astor's overland party was also facing hardships. Its leader, Wilson Price Hunt, had planned to follow Lewis and Clark's route to the Pacific Northwest. After the party had set out, Hunt learned from his men that the Blackfoot Indians on the upper Missouri were hostile to fur trappers. But the Blackfeet weren't the only ones who stood in Hunt's way.

Manuel Lisa had formed the St. Louis Fur Company (later known as the Missouri Fur Company) in 1809. He didn't want to share "his" territory, so he raced Astor's men up the Missouri. The two crews met up and guns were drawn. Faced with such obstacles, Hunt decided to travel by land instead.

That winter the men took shelter from a blizzard in an abandoned trading post near the Snake River. After the storm, they built canoes and left their horses with the friendly Shoshone. A few of their men decided to stay and trap beaver. The rest planned to travel down the Snake to the Columbia River. After losing several

> "Having an advantage of about three weeks' start, a party representing the Astor interests under the leadership of Wilson Price Hunt sought to keep well ahead of the Lisa expedition.... During two months the anxious voyageurs traveled a distance of twelve hundred miles—a feat unparalleled in the history of keelboat travel on the Missouri."
>
> *George F. Robeson, "Manuel Lisa," 1925*

crewmembers, however, they had to face the fact that the Snake could not be navigated safely.

Staying on the river was no longer an option. The crew splintered into smaller and smaller factions. It took months for all the groups to reach Fort Astoria.

Above: Manuel Lisa's house in Missouri Territory,1809
Below:A fur-trading post along the Columbia River

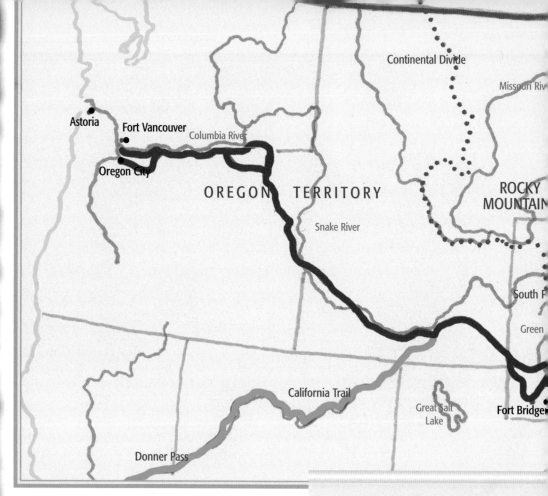

Continental Divide

Missouri Riv

Astoria

Fort Vancouver

Columbia River

Oregon City

OREGON TERRITORY

ROCKY MOUNTAIN

Snake River

South P

Green

California Trail

Great Salt Lake

Fort Bridge

Donner Pass

The Oregon Trail became famous as a route for families in covered wagons moving West in the mid-1800s. However, fur trappers were the first to travel the route. Shown here is the South Pass through the Rockies, discovered by Robert Stuart in 1812.

" [British troops] were to proceed together to the mouth of the Columbia capture or destroy whatever American fortress they should find there, and plant the British flag on its ruins."

Washington Irving, Astoria, 1836, describing the capture of Fort Astoria during the War of 1812

But life at the fort wasn't much better for Astor's men. Food was scarce. The local Indians remained hostile to trappers. And the North West Company, one of Astor's competitors, was also trapping in the area, so there was less fur to go around.

The men wanted to dispatch someone to St. Louis to tell Astor about their problems. In June of 1812, Robert Stuart left with six men. Along the way, he heard stories of an easy pass over the mountains. Stuart decided to try it.

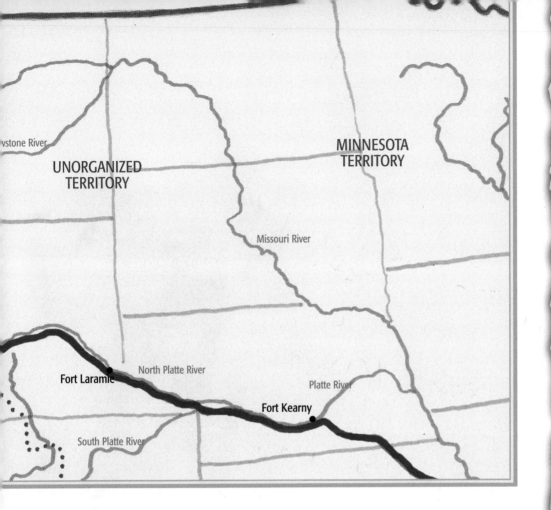

Stuart and his men reached St. Louis on April 30, 1813. It had taken them ten months, but they had discovered the South Pass, a land route from the Missouri to the Pacific. Unfortunately, this discovery was soon forgotten: By the time Stuart reached St. Louis, the United States was at war with Great Britain.

With the War of 1812, Astor's empire in Oregon crumbled. When the British arrived at Fort Astoria during the war, Astor's men sold it to them—and divided the proceeds among themselves. Astor was furious when he found out. He vowed to make back all of the money. In time, he did just that—and more.

Chapter Five

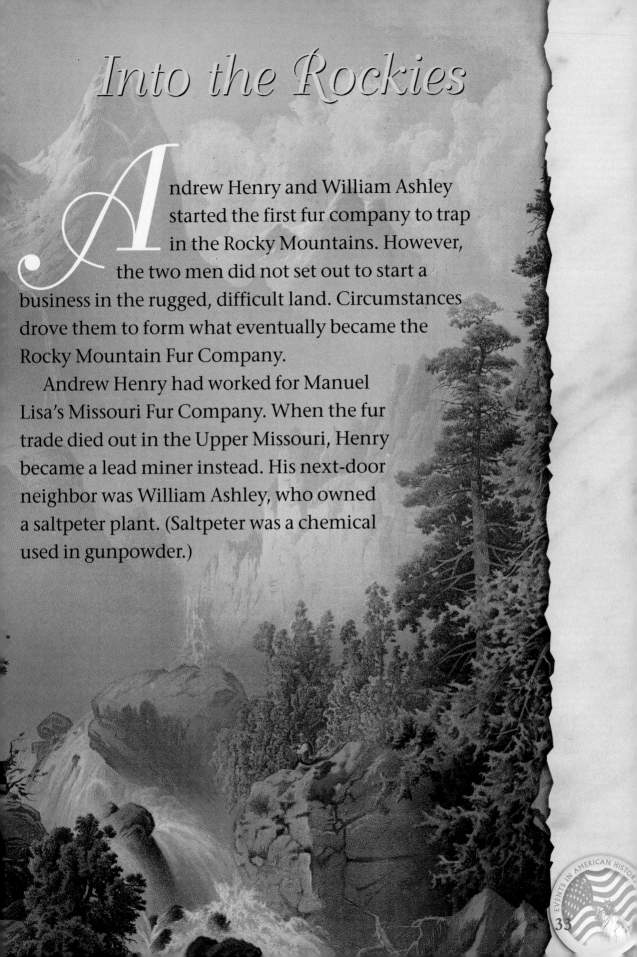

Into the Rockies

Andrew Henry and William Ashley started the first fur company to trap in the Rocky Mountains. However, the two men did not set out to start a business in the rugged, difficult land. Circumstances drove them to form what eventually became the Rocky Mountain Fur Company.

Andrew Henry had worked for Manuel Lisa's Missouri Fur Company. When the fur trade died out in the Upper Missouri, Henry became a lead miner instead. His next-door neighbor was William Ashley, who owned a saltpeter plant. (Saltpeter was a chemical used in gunpowder.)

But Henry missed the wilderness. In 1821, he and Ashley decided to form a fur company. They didn't want to rely so heavily on trading fur or building forts, so they came up with their own way of doing business. They hired men to go out into the wilderness and trap beaver themselves. This new breed of trappers became known as mountain men.

Mountain men are often remembered as rugged, courageous men.

To find workers, Ashley and Henry placed an ad in the *Missouri Gazette*. It read:

TO ENTERPRISING YOUNG MEN: THE SUBSCRIBER WISHES TO ENGAGE ONE HUNDRED MEN, TO ASCEND THE RIVER MISSOURI TO ITS SOURCE, THERE TO BE EMPLOYED FOR ONE, TWO, OR THREE YEARS.

Men came from all over to answer the ad. One of the first was Jedediah Smith. After a group of men was gathered, the trappers went upriver to trap beaver. Soon after they arrived, however, it became clear why trade on the upper Missouri had died out.

> "In the night of the third day Several of our men without permission went and remained in the village, amongst them our Interpreter Mr. Rose. About midnight he came running into camp and informed us that one of our men was killed in the village and war was declared in earnest."
>
> *James Clyman,*
> *describing a fight between*
> *trappers and Arikara Indians*

The growing fur industry had created tensions among several Indian tribes. Some, like the Sioux, simply didn't want the mountain men to trade with their enemies. Others, like the Blackfeet, didn't want them trapping on their lands. Still others, like the Arikara, had served as middlemen to traders and feared losing their position. Attacks by the Arikara were frequent, and many of Henry and Ashley's men perished. Another group of the company's trappers were killed by the Blackfoot Indians.

Ashley and Henry decided to leave the upper Missouri and head toward the Rockies. They split into two groups. Henry took his men to the Yellowstone River, and Ashley asked Jedediah Smith to lead the other group beyond it.

In September of 1823, Smith led a group of 20 men west. They headed through what is now South Dakota. They thought their troubles were finally over when they reached the Black Hills. Then a grizzly bear attacked. The bear tried to eat Smith—headfirst. By the time the men drove off the grizzly, Smith had been seriously wounded. His ear was torn off and his skull was visible where he had been bitten.

Smith wasn't going to be stopped by a bear. After another mountain man, James Clyman, stitched him up, Smith rested for a few days. Then they pressed on.

"After stitching all the other wounds in the best way I was capable and, according to the captain's directions, the ear being the last, I told him I could do nothing for his Ear. 'Oh you must try to stitch up some way or other,' said he."

James Clyman

Their next stop was a Crow village. The Crow knew one of the men and invited them to stay for the winter. Before the winter ended, however, Smith tried to lead an expedition across the Rockies. After several blizzards blocked the group's progress, they went back to live with the Crow. The Crow told them it was easier to cross the mountains farther south.

Smith took the Crow's advice when he set out on his second journey. But it was still difficult. It was too cold to sleep at night, and the winds made building a fire impossible. But this time Smith was able to cross the mountains. He traveled over the South Pass, the same route that Robert Stuart had crossed 12 years earlier.

Jedediah Smith and his men spent some winter months at a Crow Indian village like this one, illustrated in 1908.

Chapter Six

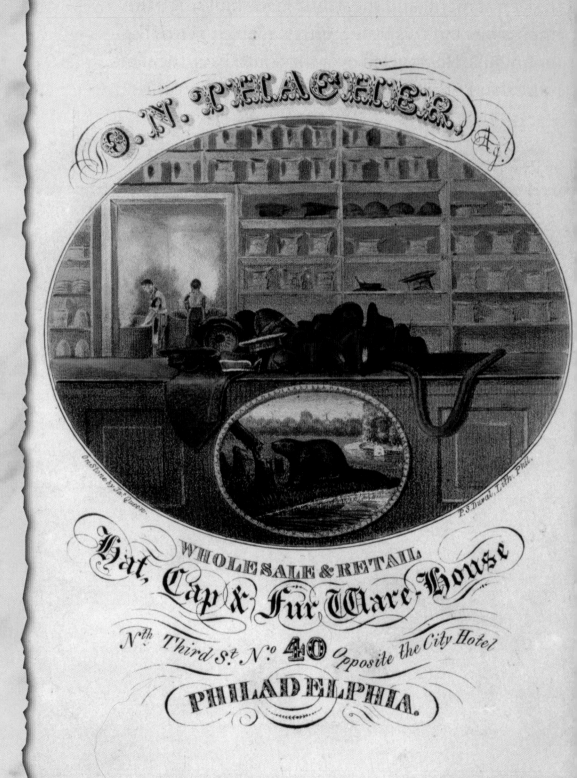

From a Beaver to a Worm

The mountain men weren't stationed at forts. Instead, they worked in small groups scattered across the Rocky Mountains throughout the year. But summer was always quiet for the men, who didn't trap in the warmest months (when a beaver's coat is thinnest). So, starting in the summer of 1825, Ashley and Henry organized an annual meeting, called a rendezvous (pronounced "RON-day-voo"). This gave them an opportunity to pay the trappers for their furs and give them supplies for the coming year.

Opposite page: An advertisement for a hat shop in Philadelphia from around 1860.
Below: In this 1904 painting, mountain men ride on horseback to gather at a summer rendezvous.

A Man of Firsts

Jedediah Smith was one of the first to answer Ashley and Henry's ad for "one hundred men." He was also the first white man to cross the South Pass going west. (When Robert Stuart did it, he was going east.)

The search for the legendary Buenaventura River added two more firsts to Smith's list. He became the first American to cross the Great Basin, a desert area in the Southwest, and reach California by land. Until that time, most travelers from the East Coast sailed around South America to reach the West Coast.

This led to Smith's becoming the first white man to travel the Pacific Coast, from California to Oregon, using a land route. This, too, had always been done by boat.

Meeting with other trappers was a treat for the mountain men. Their work was done and the weather was pleasant. The rendezvous was like a month-long party.

In the 1820s and 1830s, the mountain men continued to explore the West. In 1824, Jim Bridger became the first white person to see Utah's Great Salt Lake. Because the water was salty, Bridger thought he had reached the Pacific Ocean.

An 1874 painting shows a group on horseback admiring the Great Salt Lake of Utah. Jim Bridger first viewed the lake in 1824.

Ashley also explored the region. He wanted to find the Buenaventura, a river that had appeared on maps made by Spanish explorers in the 1700s. According to the maps, the river flowed from the Great Salt Lake to the Pacific.

From 1824 to 1826, Ashley looked for the river, but he never found it. He went back to St. Louis and retired from the fur business. Henry retired, too, and sold his share of the company to Jedediah Smith. Smith searched for the river from 1826 to 1830, but he never found it either. It simply didn't exist.

Smith's travels took him to the Pacific Ocean. He traveled north and south, between Mexico and Canada. Smith made a map of his travels, called the Fremont-Gibbs-Smith map. It was the only accurate map of the region for years.

Jim Bridger

"After the departure of the land parties, I embarked with six men on Thursday, the 21st April, on board my newly made boat and began the descent of the river."

William H. Ashley

"I wanted to be the first to view a country on which the eyes of a white man had never gazed and to follow the course of rivers that run through a new land."

Jedediah Smith

The trappers earned their living in the mountains because people in cities far away wore hats made from beaver fur. Beaver had been in demand since Europeans first arrived in North America in the fifteenth century. By the mid-nineteenth century, however, fashions had changed. Suddenly everyone wanted to wear silk hats. Silkworms were the creatures in demand now, not beavers. The market for beaver fur dried up, so the mountain men were out of a job. The last rendezvous was held in 1840. After that, the men had to find new work.

A silkworm

Because they knew the mountains so well, some mountain men became guides. Kit Carson went from trapping furs to working as a guide in the U.S. Army. Later he became an Indian agent and championed the rights of the Ute tribe. Jim Bridger set up a store along the Oregon Trail, a route first traveled by fur trappers.

The South Pass that had been discovered twice by trappers became the new doorway to the West. The maps created by mountain men were used by settlers embarking on a new life. The era of trappers and mountain men was over, but the discoveries they made helped shape a nation.

Above: A 1922 portrait of Kit Carson guiding U.S. troops across the West

"I have established a small store, with a Black Smith Shop, and a supply of Iron on the road of the Emigrants on Black's fork Green River, which promises fairly, they in coming out are generally well supplied with money, but by the time they get there are in want of all kinds of supplies."

Jim Bridger

Biographies

William Henry Ashley (1778–1838)

Ashley formed a fur company with Andrew Henry. Together they started the rendezvous in the mountains. Ashley explored the far west in his quest to find the Buenaventura River. After retiring from the fur trade, Ashley went into politics.

John Jacob Astor (1763–1848)

Astor came to the United States at age 21 with $25 and seven flutes. He created several fur companies and also worked in real estate. When he died, Astor was the richest man in the country.

Jim Bridger (1804–81)

Bridger traveled with Ashley and Henry on their first trapping expedition. Bridger was the first white person to see the Great Salt Lake. Later, Bridger opened a trading post on the Oregon Trail.

William Clark (1770–1838)

Clark was asked by Meriwether Lewis to travel with him to explore the Louisiana Purchase. Clark was second in command. Clark kept journals along the way. After Lewis's death, Clark published all their papers, along with a map he had made of their journey.

Andrew Henry (1775–1832)

Henry led many fur-trapping expeditions over the years. He began his work in the fur trade with Manuel Lisa. A few years later, Henry formed a fur company with William Ashley. Ashley and Henry's company started the summer rendezvous.

Meriwether Lewis (1774–1809)

Lewis was Thomas Jefferson's personal secretary. Jefferson asked him to lead an expedition across the land acquired in the Louisiana Purchase. Lewis and his men traveled halfway across North America to the Pacific Ocean and back. They were the first white men to do so.

Manuel Lisa (1772–1820)

Lisa worked as a fur trader in New Orleans. After Lewis and Clark returned from their expedition, he formed the St. Louis Fur Company and began trapping on the Upper Missouri. He also built the first outpost in that area, Fort Raymond.

Sacagawea (ca. 1787–1812)

Sacagawea was kidnapped at age 12 and taken to a Hidatsa village in what is now North Dakota. She married the French Canadian trader, Toussaint Charbonneau. After her son, Jean Baptiste Charbonneau, was born, the entire family traveled with the Corps of Discovery.

Jedediah Strong Smith (1799–1831)

Smith was one of the first to answer Ashley and Henry's ad for "one hundred men." Smith rediscovered the South Pass. After buying out Ashley's share in the Rocky Mountain Fur Company, Smith traveled extensively in the West. He was the first white man to cross the Great Basin, a large desert area covering present-day Nevada and parts of neighboring states.

Timeline

July 1803
With the Louisiana Purchase, the size of the United States is more than doubled.

1803

May 1804
Lewis and Clark leave from a town near St. Louis, Missouri.

September 23, 1806
Lewis and Clark return to St. Louis.

April 19, 1807
Manuel Lisa meets John Colter on the Missouri.

September 8, 1810
John Jacob Astor sends a ship to the Pacific Northwest.

October 23, 1812
Robert Stuart discovers the South Pass.

October 1813
Fort Astoria is sold to the North West Company.

February 13, 1822
Ashley and Henry advertise for trappers.

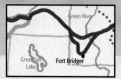

March 1824
Jedediah Smith rediscovers the South Pass.

1840

Summer of 1840
The last fur-trading rendezvous is held.

Glossary

corps (CORE)
a group of specially trained people working together for a specific purpose

empire (EHM-pyr)
a large company or group of companies under one owner

expedition (EX-puh-DISH-uhn)
a group traveling together to work for the same goal

felt (FEHLT)
a fabric of matted, compressed animal fibers, such as wool or fur

flint (FLIHNT)
a piece of quartz (a hard mineral) that makes a spark when struck against steel and can be used to start a fire

foe (FOH)
an enemy

geyser (GY-zuhr)
a spring that shoots hot water and steam out of the ground from time to time

hatter (HAT-uhr)
someone who makes and sells hats

hostile (HOS-tuhl)
feeling or showing ill will, as toward an enemy

perish (PEHR-ish)
to die or be destroyed, especially in a violent or untimely manner

rendezvous (RON-day-voo)
a meeting at a prearranged time and place

Further Resources

Web Links

Inside the Corps

www.pbs.org/lewisandclark/inside/index.html

Based on a PBS show about Lewis and Clark, "Inside the Corps" has three sections: Circa 1803 (historical context), To Equip an Expedition, and the Corps (biographies).

Mountain Men and the Fur Trade

www.xmission.com/~drudy/amm.html

This Web site is an online research center devoted to the history, traditions, tools, and mode of living of the trappers, explorers, and traders known as the mountain men. The "library" has books on the mountain men, including their diaries, narratives, and letters.

White Oak Society, Inc.

http://www.whiteoak.org/index.shtml

White Oak Society is a nonprofit organization providing living-history interpretations of the fur trade within the Great Lakes region, specifically of 1798 Minnesota.

Books

Glass, Andrew. *Mountain Men: True Grit and Tall Tales*. Doubleday Books for Young Readers, 2001.

Nelson, Sharlene, and Ted Nelson. *Jedediah Smith*. Franklin Watts, 2004.

Sundling, Charles W. *Mountain Men of the Frontier*. Abdo & Daughters, 2000.

Index